GW00367811

Jaroslav Weigel

The Dog's Dinner

Recipes so good that *you* can eat the leftovers

EBURY PRESS
LONDON

Dedicated to Feda Subava and Anna de Vratenberk

1 3 5 7 9 10 8 6 4 2

Illustrations by Jaroslav Weigel
Text and artwork copyright © Paseka, 1992
Cover photo © Miroslav Zajic, 1992

First published in Czech by Paseka, Prague in 1992, and in Spanish by Edouard Cointreau S.P.A, Madrid in 1996.

First published in the United Kingdom in 1997 by Ebury Press
Random House · 20 Vauxhall Bridge Road · London SW1V 2SA

Random House Australia (Pty) Limited
20 Alfred Street, Milsons Point · Sydney · New South Wales 2061 · Australia

Random House New Zealand Limited
18 Poland Road · Glenfield · Auckland 10 · New Zealand

Random House South Africa (Pty) Limited
Endulini · 5A Jubilee Road · Parktown 2193 · South Africa

Random House UK Limited Reg. No. 954009

A catalogue record for this book is available from the British Library

ISBN: 0 09 185371 0

Designed by Lovelock & Co.
Printed and bound in Portugal by Printer Portuguesa, Lisbon

CONTENTS

A little plea on behalf of our most faithful friends who need not only our love, but – as decreed by Mother Nature – tasty food as well.

Prague, November 1992

Introduction

E very day, at any time, you will be welcomed by a most faithful friend – your dog. He barks joyfully, jumps up and down and waits to be praised. When you arrive home tired and fed up, he is there at the door to greet you, happy that you are home at last after his long day alone. He tells you that life is not really as bad as it seems and he is always there ready with his love and devotion. And you will bend down and stroke him, and your mood changes and the world will suddenly becomes a better place. As a reward for this, and many other delightful moments, it is worth giving up a little time to cook for him and invite him to the dinner you have prepared for him.

In these days of tinned dog food and ready-mixes, we would like to offer this little book of advice and recipes so that he can enjoy a little home cooking.

What we put in our best friend's bowl

Before writing *The Dogs Dinner*, I handed a short questionnaire to friends, acquaintances and other dog-owners. First I asked for answers to the basic questions (type of breed, weight, sex and age) and then enquired about their dogs' diets. I was interested in discovering the quantity of food they gave their dogs daily, the dogs' favourite treats, any special recipes as well as the ratio of raw meat to vegetables etc. The questions were intended for the owners of healthy, fully-grown dogs who are (or ought to be) fed once a day.

I was surprised by the enthusiastic responses of those I asked. I received back 128 completed questionnaires. Of these, I selected the hundred or so which seemed to me to have taken my questions seriously.

They made interesting and often surprising reading, with sad and funny moments. A good two-thirds of all our 'Fidos' and 'Rovers' are considered by their owners to be meat-eaters who have become omnivorous through domestication. Their masters and mistresses understand that they need both meat and vegetable protein, fats and carbohydrates. The replies showed that the variety of food was good, but the level of calorie consumption was not always appropriate.

The most common food was beef, followed by offal, and then poultry. Fish appeared less frequently. However, the quantity of meat often greatly exceeded the quantity of supplementary foods. Many dogs appeared to be overfed. When dogs are given too much red meat or offal, they are susceptible to diarrhoea.

The meat was usually supplemented with pasta and grains, especially macaroni, wheat flakes, rolled oats and groats. Only one third of those questioned gave their adult dogs cheese, cottage cheese or yoghurt. Several dog-owners (mostly those who owned lap dogs) gave their pets milk. Though dogs may be attracted to milk by its smell, it can often be another cause of diarrhoea.

Regular mineral and vitamin supplements were very rarely given.

The amount of fruit and vegetables given to dogs food was gratifying. The most popular vegetables were carrots, and apples topped the fruit list. Lettuce, finely-chopped dandelion leaves and young nettles were often given to dogs. Choosy dogs might prefer cauliflower, kohlrabi or a cabbage stalk. Even tomato or cucumber were not refused. Some dogs picked their own strawberries, raspberries and bilberries. There was even a dog which liked onion, but only when cooked with brawn. Such a dog does not necessarily deserve praise, although the vegetable and fruit 'gourmets' do.

Raw meat was either not served or was refused by approximately a third of the dogs. We recommend their masters try Recipe No. 3.

Most owners agreed that a healthy adult dog should be fed once a day, usually in the evening. At the same time, most admitted that their pets were given titbits throughout the day.

Twenty-one owners out of the hundred considered their dogs to be omnivorous, sharing what the human pack ate that day or getting left-overs from family and human friends. This way, they got to know the menus of their neighbours, school or restaurant kitchens and the like. Such food is often strongly spiced, salty or burned and thus not suitable for a dog's stomach.

Three village dogs were given scraps, often consisting only of bread soaked in warm water, the sort of slops reminiscent of pig food. That is a sad state of affairs.

Two owners of large dogs held the view that a dog is just a carnivore and that is that. Their dogs were given raw meat, often of poor quality, which was thrown to them in a lump. They are absolutely wrong in considering this approach to feeding to be natural. I would not like to be their dog.

Replies about dogs' favourite titbits were impressively varied. The winner for small and medium dogs was liver pâté, followed very closely by York ham, brawn, salami and sausages of all kinds. Some owners confessed to their dogs being dependent on chocolate and cakes. A miniature poodle was wild about vanilla ice cream, and a chow-chow would only eat home-baked cakes, refusing the shop-bought variety. Raw dough seemed to be a favourite with some, and there were others who stole the cat's food. Despite the fact that most owners were perfectly well aware of the harm done to their dogs by giving them human treats, they still gave in to their pets from to time to time. They shouldn't do this, because it shortens a dog's life. Much more to my liking were the ascetic schnauzer Bondy and the basset Pecka, both of whom had a preference for stale bread rolls.

The dalmatian who was able to bone a kipper perfectly deserves praise, if only for his skill.

Recipes for special dishes appeared in replies in twenty-four out of the hundred questionnaires. Most of them revealed above all the master's love for his pet but, unfortunately, not enough attention was paid to healthy and suitable nutrition. A recipe such as Mrs. R's for Beef Olives Stuffed with Chicken could not be included due to cost in time and money. Maybe I will cook it for myself one day! For health reasons I must reject recipes for 'special occasions', such as the sponge cake decorated with whipped cream and stoned cherries, or the cocoa balls made with rolled oats (I'd prefer not to mention the others). I rejected the Pasta and Salami Salad, risotto made with cured meat, steaks stewed in beer, or a whole list of fried foods. 'Rolf's favourite', made from smoked ham knuckle, has also been excluded.

On the other hand, slimming Recipe No. 4 and low-calorie Recipe No. 22 are worth special consideration. I adjusted the quantities as well as the protein, fat and carbohydrate content of some of the other recipes included.

Many recipes contained mistakes in the preparation of food such as rolled oats and offal. Salt and spices were often added; potatoes, which are difficult for dogs to digest, were served too often. However, small amounts of mashed potato can be beneficial for dogs who need to watch their weight.

The recipe (No. 1) submitted by Mrs. Malková for Boiled Beef with Rice, Vegetables and Egg was most suitable. Though I have no doubt this basic dish is known by everyone, we can still find several interesting details in it.

Processed dog food, such as dog food in tins, granulated foodstuffs and complete food mixes come in a wide variety of mixtures. The advantage of this food is its balanced composition, including mineral and vitamin supplements, as well as its quick preparation. One owner had gradually changed over from home cooking to the use of this complete food for his Irish terrier. See Recipe No. 8. We can agree with such a change. However, eight owners went over too suddenly to using tinned or dried food, especially during weekends or when on holiday. According to expert opinion, this is harmful to the dog's digestion. These owners should make a clear choice, either to use the quick complete dried food, or to spend some time on home cooking.

Only twelve owners had created a menu-planning system for periods longer than a day. After some adjustments, menu plans have been included in *The Dog's Dinner*, based on the recipes in this book. The other owners relied either on leftovers from the refrigerator, or on random purchases, or on 'pot luck'.

The questionnaire was a very important guide for me. I would therefore like to thank all my friends and acquaintances who very readily and frankly replied to all my prying questions. Thank you.

Regards from Man, the dog's best friend.

The Art of the Table

Dog food is best served in ceramic bowls. Two are needed, one for water and one for food. They should be heavy enough to ensure that the dog does not have to 'chase' them around the room.

A healthy, adult dog should be fed once a day. The best time is in the evening after a walk outside. After coming home, let the dog rest for a while and then serve him his food. As a rule, he will eat it with relish, and then lie down quickly to digest it. It is my experience that the best time to take a dog out for a walk is 5.30 p.m. Let him have a rest before serving him his supper at 6.30 p.m. and then take him out again for a short walk around 10.00 p.m.

Try to serve his food at the same time and in the same place each day.

Do not forget that a dog should always have access to clean water at room temperature.

Our friend's food should be thick in consistency, resembling a well-mixed mash rather than a thin soup.

You can feed your dog at the same time as the family eats the evening meal. However, it is better to serve your dog his food before the family eats as this will ensure he can eat in peace.

Do not talk to your dog or pet him while he eats. The

day's food should disappear from the bowl with nothing left over. A well-licked bowl is proof of the satisfaction of your friend and, last but not least, of your culinary skill.

It is a good idea to watch your dog discreetly while he is eating. He should eat with obvious enjoyment. The bowl should be taken away when it is empty and he has left it. Usually it takes him no more than ten minutes. Small dogs, who are often unable to eat all their daily ration at one session, should have food served to them twice a day. The same applies to old and sick dogs.

If a dog leaves a small amount of food in the bowl, the quantity should be reduced the next day. However, leaving a negligible portion is not necessarily a sign that a dog is ill, simply that you may have been too generous.

Should you observe that the dog is eating his usual ration without enjoyment, do not worry immediately. Keep an eye on his behaviour, as this may be a temporary aberration, and next day everything should be back to normal.

However, if a dog refuses for more than two days running food which he previously liked, ask the vet for advice.

Serving the remains from your own plate to your friend is not good for both aesthetic and hygienic reasons. It is also a good idea to keep a separate fork, spoon, ladle and wooden spoon for cooking food for your dog away from your normal set of cooking utensils.

WHAT YOU SHOULD KNOW

1 Food which a dog needs for nutrition, to replace lost energy and for his healthy development consists of **animal proteins and fats** (beef, offal, fish, egg, cottage cheese, hard cheese etc.). The 'side-dishes' consist of sources of **vegetable protein**, **vegetable fats and carbohydrates**, such as sugar, starch and cellulose (foods such as pasta, rice, oats, wheat and soya, pearl barley, wholemeal bread and bread rolls, boiled and raw vegetables etc.). Your vet will recommend the right amount and combination of **mineral and vitamin supplements**.

2 **The daily ration of food**, the size of which should be determined by the workload of the dog (hunting, training etc.), its opportunities for exercise (walks, roaming in the garden etc.), age, breed characteristics, environment (indoors or outside etc.), whether the animal is a bitch in pup or nursing etc. The following data on the amount, composition and daily energy requirement, including coefficients, have been reproduced from the book about dog breeding by Dr Zdeněk Procházka, the Czech veterinarian.

3 The daily food ration should range between **30–60 g /1–2 oz per kilogram/2¼ lbs** of the dog's weight (see point 2).

4 **Composition of the daily food:** for each 1 kg/2¼ lbs of the dog's weight, a minimum of 4.4 g proteins, a minimum 1.3 g fat and a maximum 10.1 g of carbohydrates (sugars).

5 **Daily energy requirement:** for each kg/2¼ lbs of the dog's weight:

1–5 kg/2¼–11 lbs	460 kJ/110 Kcal
5–10 kg/11–22 lbs	350 kJ/85 Kcal
10–20 kg/22–44 lbs	287 kJ/70 Kcal*

6 **Additional energy requirement ratio:** a dog living under a tough regime who is constantly active (such as a police-dog), ratio of 2.0–4.0.
A pregnant bitch in her first 3–6 weeks: 1.5–2.0.
A pregnant bitch in her seventh week after whelping: 1.2–1.5.
A nursing bitch in her first or second week after whelping: 2.0–3.0.
A nursing bitch in her third to fifth week after whelping: 3.0–4.0.
A breeding dog: 1.2–2.0.

*The daily energy and nutritional requirements of a puppy are double the above.

BEFORE YOU START TO COOK ANY OF THE RECIPES

1 First of all you need to know the correct weight of your dog. Consult a breeder or a vet to make sure your dog is not overweight or even underweight.

2 **Weigh your dog**. The easiest way is to weigh yourself with your dog in your arms. Then weigh yourself without the dog, but do not step off the scales while doing so or the result will not be correct. You may also weigh your dog at the veterinary surgery.

3 **Recipes give the weight of cooked food.** Do not forget that:

a The original weight of meat decreases by one third when boiled. For example you would have to boil 150 g/5½ oz of raw beef to get 100 g/3½ oz of boiled beef.

b Cooked rice weighs three times as much as raw rice: (50–150 g/1¾–5½ oz)

c Cooked pasta also weighs three times as much as uncooked (30–90 g/1–3 oz).

d Porridge weighs five times as much as raw oatmeal (10–50 g/¼–1¾ oz).

Obviously the weight of raw meat must be taken as approximate. The decrease in weight depends on the quality of the meat, the method of preparation and how long it is allowed to cook. The same applies to offal which loses more than one third of its original weight through cooking. Non-meat supplements behave differently in cooking. However, here too are some variations (for example, pasta varies according to quality, size and composition) and preparing starchy foods the wrong way can often make a difference. Pasta should be left to stand after boiling. Rice should be well cooked.

4 Each recipe consists of the following:
a   A basic recipe for a dog weighing l5 kg/33 lbs, including quantities of the ingredients.
b   Method of food preparation.
c   Breakdown for dogs of different weights.
d   Evaluation of the food.

The weight of the cooked food in the recipes is printed in bold type.

5 Weighing food for little dogs of various sizes can be problematic, so here is a measuring system using teaspoons or tablespoons.

Uncooked weights

1 level teaspoon	rice	3 g
	pasta	3 g
	rolled oats	2 g
1 rounded teaspoon	rice	6 g
	pasta	4 g
	rolled oats	4 g
1 level tablespoon	rice	8 g
	pasta	7 g
	rolled oats	5 g
1 rounded tablespoon	rice	12 g
	pasta	10 g
	rolled oats	10 g
1 level teaspoon of	fat	5 g

Of course this method is not exact, and one would need to be a chemist to work out the exact weights for little dogs. There is an easier way, which is to cook double portions, so that the rest can be stored in the refrigerator for another time. When cooking for a dog, a sensible cook thinks of himself or herself. So if you cook risotto with vegetables or pasta baked with ham and Parmesan cheese or porridge with sultanas and fruit juice, you and your pet could eat the same cooked food. All it takes is a little imagination.

As for meat and offal, I recommend a tried and tested method. Both should be bought in larger quantities, cooked, divided into daily rations and frozen. It is important to remove a portion from the freezer well before you need it so that it has plenty of time to thaw. Then heat and add the prepared additions.

6 **Calculating the weight** of the various ingredients within the weight categories is simple.

a For a dog weighing 2–5 kg/4½–11 lbs:
The difference in weight should be divided by three as this gives the amount of food required per 1 kg/2¼ lbs of the dog's weight.
For example, if your dog weighs 4 kg/9 lbs how much meat will he need?
At the end of each recipe you will find a table of the weights of each of the ingredients. A dog in the 2 kg/4½ lbs category should get 25g/1 oz boiled meat, and one in the 5 kg/11 lb category 75 g/2¾ oz boiled meat. The difference is 75 g/2¾ oz minus 30 g/1 oz = 45 g /1¾ oz boiled meat. 45 g/1¾ oz divided by three = 15 g/½ oz (this is the addition per 1 kg/ 2¼ lbs of the dog's weight).
A 4 kg/9 lb dog should be given four times more, i.e. 60 g/2¼ oz boiled meat.

b The weight of food for other weight categories (5 kg /11 lbs or more) can be arrived at by the same calculation, but the difference between the lower and higher ends of the weight range should be divided by five.

If your dog weighs 8 kg/17¾ lbs he is in the 5–10 kg /11–22-lb weight category. So, for instance, in the case of rice:

A dog in the 5 kg/11 lbs category should get 60 g/2¼ oz rice; a dog weighing 10 kg/22 lbs should get 120 g/4 oz rice.

120 g minus 60 g = 60 g/5 or 4¼ oz minus 2¼ oz = 2 oz. This divided by 5 = 12 g/⅝ oz of boiled rice per 1 kg/2¼ lbs weight of dog.

An 8 kg/17¾ lb dog should receive eight times more boiled rice, i.e., 96 g/3⅝ oz.

These results can be rounded up to make weighing easier (for example, 96 g/3⅝ oz to 100 g/3½ oz). Many of these sums can be worked out in the head, but the above calculations may help those owners who have less experience.

7 The recipes in *The Dog's Dinner* have been devised in order to conform as closely as possible to the recommended daily requirements for proteins, fat, carbohydrates and energy. The recipes are based

mainly on the minimum weight of food required (that is 30 g:1 kg/1 oz: 2¼ lbs of body weight of the dog) and correct protein intake. The weight of the food is mainly increased by vegetables, considered to be an important constituent of a balanced canine diet.

The quantities in these recipes are intended for moderately active, fully grown dogs. However, the quantities are only a recommendation and do not necessarily have to be strictly followed. If your dog weighs less than he ought, you should increase his food proportionately. If your dog is older or overweight through lack of exercise, then it is better to decrease the amount of food. For instance, you may find that your 8 kg/17½ lb fox terrier can be fed the same as a 10 kg/22 lb dog without getting fat. On the other hand, an 11-year-old schnauzer, weighing 20 kg/44 lbs, might be satisfied with a ration suitable for a dog weighing only 15 kg/33 lbs.

NOTE When you study the recipes more carefully you will notice that the ratio of meat to other foods is 1:1. This is the general recommendation from the breeders of adult dogs. These quantities are not suitable for young dogs, for whom the ratio of meat to other foods should be 2:1, or for older dogs for whom the ratio of meat and supplements should only be 1:2.

It should be remembered that the adult age differs for various breeds. In general, the majority of dogs can be said to have reached adulthood when they have finished growing, which is about the age of 18 months.

8 **A reminder which must not be overlooked:** The recipe ingredients, choice of food and proportions are suitable for dogs weighing up to 22 kg/48½ lbs at the most. For heavier weight categories, the calorific values need to be higher and more proteins and fats are needed. The food plan for larger dogs requires different ratios and in many cases the quality does not need to be so high, so that lower-quality meat and cheaper offal can be used. Cooking methods should be changed as well, for example by combining meat, offal and various grains. Any essential nutrients can be compensated for by adding supplements to the diet. However, *The Dog's Dinner* does not cover this.

9 **Most important:** You are the best judge of how much to give your dog. You know your dog best and you can judge his vigour, performance or lack of energy. You are most familiar with his environment, habits and appetite. Remember points 2 and 6 in the section 'What you should know' on pages 14–15. But watch his weight and he will be all the better for it.

The Recipes

Boiled Beef (forequarter), Rice, Vegetables and Egg

For a dog weighing 15 kg/33 lbs:
220 g/7½ oz boiled beef, **180 g/6½ oz** boiled rice,
60 g/2¼ oz boiled root vegetables, two eggs.

Put 330 g/11½ oz washed raw meat into cold, slightly salted, water. Bring to the boil and simmer for about 30 minutes, depending on the quality of the meat. It should remain slightly tough rather than overcooked. It will lose approximately one third of its weight. Any foam rising to the surface of the water should be added to the soup.

While the soup is cooking, cook the rice, using your favourite method. I usually rinse it under hot water and then put it into cold, unsalted water, using one-third rice to two-thirds water. Then I bring it to the boil and cook it for 11 minutes. When cooked, rice should be left to stand for several minutes and then strained. The rice should treble in bulk. Pre-cooked rice can also be used.

At the same time, prepare the vegetables. Frozen vegetables are suitable and they take one-third less time to prepare. Cook the vegetables in as little water as possible. Cover the pot with a lid and bring the water to the boil quickly. When the water boils, reduce the heat and simmer the vegetables until just soft. Do not overcook.

Cut the beef into dog-bite-sized pieces. They should be just large enough to enable the dog to chew comfortably. He can then digest them properly and will feel satisfied.

Put the pieces of meat into the dog's bowl, adding the rice. The cooked vegetables can be mashed with a fork on a wooden chopping-board and then added to the bowl. Everything should be mixed thoroughly. Break the two eggs, whisk them, and mix them with a little of the hot stock, then add them to the bowl. Add the rest of the vegetables or beef stock and stir to make a thick mash. Finally, add any mineral and vitamin supplements.

The rest of the beef stock can be stored in the refrigerator. Vegetable stock should not be kept for more than two days, otherwise it loses its food value.

A hungry dog should not be given bones because he will swallow pieces which could harm his digestive organs. Give them to him after food, so that he has time to chew them in a leisurely way for enjoyment rather than to satisfy his hunger.

He who gives bread to another man's dog,
will lose the bread and lose the dog

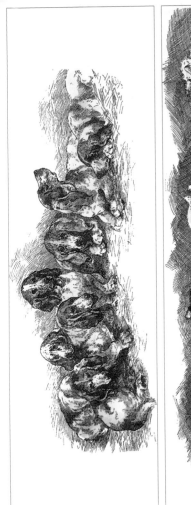

Man is a dog's best friend

At the end of her recipe, Mrs. Malíková recommends making double portions. One half to be served on Friday and the second on Sunday evening with the addition of fresh pasta after returning from a weekend away.

2 kg/4½ lbs:
30 g/1⅛ oz meat, **25 g/1oz rice**, **10 g/¼ oz** vegetables, ½ an egg. During the day 10 g/¼ oz yellow cheese and 2 dog biscuits.

5 kg/11 lbs:
70 g/2½ oz meat, **60 g/2¼ oz** rice, **30 g/1⅛ oz** vegetables, one egg. During the day another 15 g/½ oz yellow cheese, 3–4 dog biscuits.

Here it should be added that the breakdown of the meals corresponds to the nutritional needs for dogs in the lower weight categories, but it does not take into account energy consumption (calories). This could be adjusted by additional food given during the day, but this is unnecessary. Little dogs, in particular, have a tendency to grow fat. If the supplement is to replace loss of fats or proteins, then it should be given. The symbol 🦴 is used in the recipes to indicate this addition.

10 kg/22 lbs:
150 g/5½ oz meat, **120 g/4¼ oz** rice, **50 g/1¾ oz** vegetables, one egg.
🦴 during the day a slice of hard cheese (20 g/¾ oz).

15 kg/33 lbs:
220 g/7½ oz meat, **180 g/6½ oz** rice, **60 g/2¼ oz** vegetables, two eggs.

20 kg/44 lbs:
300 g/10½ oz meat, **250 g/9 oz** rice, **70 g/2½ oz** vegetables, two eggs.*

Dogs weighing **20–22 kg/44–50 lbs**, can be given, for each additional 1 kg/2¼ lbs of body weight: **10 g/¼ oz** meat, **10 g/¼ oz** rice, **10 g/¼ oz** vegetables, 2 eggs (but no more).

The meal contains all the nutrients needed. For the 15 kg/33 lbs weight category this meal is richer in calories. Do not forget to 'clean teeth' after a meal (give your dog a dog biscuit, a piece of carrot or apple, or a piece of stale bread).

---

* Raw eggs should not appear very often in the dog's menu. Egg white contains avidin which interferes with the absorption of Vitamin B. That is why eggs used here are boiled or baked, as an addition or garnish only (see Recipe No. 19). Raw egg yolk is suitable, especially for the nutrition of puppies. Well-boiled egg shells can also be added to the diet (see Recipe No. 25).

RECIPE No. 2

Boiled Beef (forequarter), Pasta, Lettuce, Rolled Oats

For a dog weighing 15 kg/33 lbs:
200 g/7 oz boiled beef, **240 g/8½ oz** boiled pasta, lettuce (young nettles or fresh dandelion leaves), 2 tablespoons of rolled oats or wheat flakes.

Boil the beef as in Recipe No. 1. Put the pasta into plenty of boiling water, about 500 ml/18 fl oz. Stir the pasta and bring to the boil. Cooking time will depend on the size of the pasta. Follow the manufacturer's instructions.

The boiled pasta should be left covered with a kitchen towel for several minutes to soften. Then drain and rinse under hot water. The volume of pasta should have increased and its weight should have trebled.

If using oats*, place them in the bowl first. Then pour a little hot stock over them before adding the other ingredients.

A large portion of bones can cause constipation. Chicken and rabbit bones splinter and are therefore dangerous.

Cut up the meat, add the pasta and the finely shredded lettuce leaves. Finally, pour the rest of the stock over the dish, taking care to keep a good, thick consistency.

2 kg/4½ lbs:
30 g/1⅛ oz meat, **30 g/1⅛ oz** pasta**, lettuce leaves, heaped teaspoon of rolled oats.

🦴 During the day ⅓ small tub of cream cheese.

5 kg/11 lbs:
70 g/2½ oz meat, **60 g/2¼ oz** pasta, lettuce or other raw green vegetables, 1 heaped teaspoon rolled oats

🦴 During the day ½ small tub of cream cheese.

10 kg/22 lbs:
130 g/4½ oz meat, **130 g/4½ oz** pasta, lettuce or green leaves, 1½ heap tablespoons rolled oats.

🦴 During the day ½ small tub of cream cheese.

* Uncooked rolled oats are not only a source of roughage to encourage good bowel movement. When cooked, they become an important source of nutrition and energy.
** Little dogs should be given small pieces of pasta. This pasta can also be measured correctly with a spoon. For example, for 30 g/1⅛ oz boiled pasta you will need 10 g/¼ oz raw pasta. (This is equivalent to one rounded tablespoon of small-size pasta.)

15 kg/33 lbs:
200 g/7 oz meat, **200 g/7 oz** pasta, lettuce or green leaves, 2 heaped tablespoons of rolled oats.

🦴 Try to replace the fats and proteins used up during the day by serving ½ small tub of cream cheese. Do not exceed this amount or it may result in excessive calorie consumption.

20 kg/44 lbs:
270 g/9¼ oz meat, **270 g/9¼ oz** pasta, lettuce or green leaves, 2 heaped tablespoons of rolled oats.

🦴 During the day a small modest snack: ½ small tub of cream cheese.

20–22 kg/44–50 lbs:
10 g/¼ oz meat per 1kg/2¼ lbs of body weight, **5 g/⅛ oz** pasta and ⅕ small tub of cream cheese.

Many dogs are not accustomed to eating raw meat, although it is a source of important nutrients which are destroyed by cooking. To preserve these essential nutrients, try Recipe No. 3.

> NOTE You may have noticed that using pasta, which is richer in protein and fats than rice, means that you need less beef (see Recipe No. 1).

RECIPE No. 3

Beef (stewing steak), Pasta, Vegetables

For a dog weighing 15 kg/33 lbs:

200 g/7 oz raw stewing steak, **200 g/7 oz** boiled pasta, **50 g/1¾ oz** boiled root vegetables.

First prepare the pasta as in the previous recipe. Cook the vegetables in a larger quantity of water this time as the vegetable stock will be used later.

When the pasta is ready and resting under a tea-towel and the vegetables have been cooked, it is time to prepare the meat. This does not take long.

Pour 750 ml/27 fl oz slightly salted water into a pot and heat it. Cut the meat, which should be of good quality, into smaller pieces than the dog is accustomed to when eating it boiled. Put the meat on a plate. Watch the water carefully and before it reaches boiling point (when bubbles start to rise from the bottom) add the meat. Watch it until it becomes pale in colour and the juices are sealed in. This will take a very short time. Do not let the water come to the boil. Strain the meat through a sieve. The meat will still be pink and bloody inside and will not have lost much weight. Use only the sediment from the bottom of the pan and discard the rest of the water *.

Now mix the meat and pasta with the vegetables. The mixture can be moistened with some vegetable stock. As usual, serve it warm and of a fairly thick consistency. Do not forget the vitamin and mineral supplements.

2 kg/4½ lbs:
35 g/1¼ oz meat, **30 g/1⅛ oz** small size pasta, one tablespoon cooked root vegetables (**10 g/¼ oz**).

During the day 3-4 dog biscuits.

5 kg/11 lbs:
80 g/2⅞ oz meat, **60 g/2¼ oz** pasta, **30 g/1⅛ oz** root vegetables.

During the day ½ slice of stale bread.

10 kg/22 lbs:
130 g/4½ oz meat, **140 g/5 oz** pasta, **40 g/1½ oz** root vegetables.

15 kg/33 lbs:
200 g/7 oz meat, **200 g/7 oz** pasta, **50 g/1¾ oz** root vegetables.

20 kg/44 lbs:
250 g/9 oz meat, **270 g/9¼ oz** pasta, **80 g/2⅞ oz** root vegetables.

* Alternatively you can shallow-fry the meat in a little fat for a short time. Add the juices to the moistening liquid.

20–22 kg/44–50 lbs:

For each 1 kg/2¼ lbs of body weight, add **10 g/¼ oz meat, 15 g/ ½ oz** pasta and **15 g/½ oz** root vegetables.

This recipe is rich in fats and calories (and thus especially suitable for dogs weighing more than 10 kg/22 lbs). Serve after a rather plain dish or during periods of increased activity.

An example of a plain dish is Recipe No. 4 which is also suitable when the dog is dieting.

NOTE Raw meat contains the bacteria which causes toxoplasmosis. It is therefore better to store the meat in the freezer for 3–5 days at –20° C/–4°F before using. If you feed a dog raw meat, which you can do occasionally, it is better to hand him small pieces, one at a time.

RECIPE No. 4

Beef, Mashed Potato, Rice (plain, diet food)

For a dog weighing 15 kg/33 lbs:
150 g/5½ oz lean boiled beef (forequarter), **150 g/5½ oz** boiled potatoes, **150 g/5½ oz** boiled rice.

First, boil the beef (after cutting off any fat) as described in Recipe No. 1. Boiling potatoes is a simple matter so there is no need to describe the method. We also know how to boil rice from Recipe No. 1.

Mash the potatoes to a fairly thin consistency (adding water or stock). Cut up the boiled meat and mix it with the rice and mashed potato. Add chopped parsley. It is not necessary to add stock. Serve warm to your friend.

This is a meal for dogs on a diet. It has a reduced protein, fat, carbohydrate and calorie content and is recommended for sick, old or obese dogs. The ration can be divided into two parts: half the meat can be mixed with mashed potatoes (you can add a small amount of root vegetables too). The other half can be served with rice and parsley.

You will certainly have noticed that the breakdown of the basic recipe for dog weight categories is very simple.

According to the dog's body weight, divide the ingredients into thirds (one third meat, one third mashed potato and one third rice). Only 30 g/1⅛ oz of food should be given per 1 kg/2¼ lbs.

RECIPE No. 5

Chicken, Porridge, Rice

For a dog weighing 15 kg/33 lbs:
200 g/7 oz boiled chicken, **100 g/3½ oz** porridge, **90 g/3¼ oz** boiled rice.

Put a chicken portion into slightly salted water and boil until soft, or rather until the meat can be separated from the bones. At the same time, cook the rice. Now make the porridge. Put 20 g/¾ oz, an apparently small portion, of porridge oats into water. Use five times more water than oats. Boil, stirring occasionally over low heat for about 5 minutes, or until thickened. If the porridge thickens too soon, thin it with a little water.

Drain the boiled chicken and remove the bones. Cut

Although you have given your dog a sufficient quantity of food, he may sometimes appear hungry or even underfed. This is our fault, because the food we give him may not contain the necessary nutrients. This does not depend on the amount of food, but rather on its structure.

the meat, with any cartilage, into small pieces. Mix the porridge in a bowl with the rice. Add the meat and a little stock. You can improve the quality of the food by adding young dandelion leaves or lettuce. Mix well and serve it to your friend.

2 kg/4½ lbs:

30 g/1⅛ oz chicken meat, **25 g/1 oz** porridge oats, **10 g/¼ oz** rice. During the day an active dog may be given ¼ of a small tub of cream cheese.

5 kg/11 lbs:

80 g/2⅞ oz chicken, **50 g/1¾ oz** porridge oats, **30 g/1⅛ oz** rice. During the day you may give ⅓ of a small tub of cream cheese.

10 kg/22 lbs:

150 g/5½ oz chicken meat, **75 g/2¾ oz** porridge oats, **60 g/2¼ oz** rice.

15 kg/33 lbs:

200 g/7 oz chicken meat, **100 g/3½ oz** porridge, **90 g/3¼ oz** rice.

20 kg/44 lbs:

280 g/9⅞ oz chicken meat, **150 g/5½ oz** porridge, **120 g/4¼ oz** rice

NOTE The chicken can, of course, be grilled or roasted and used for your own needs. You can then give the leftovers to your dog.

20–22 kg/44–50 lbs:
15 g/½ oz chicken meat, a minimum quantity of porridge and rice per 1 kg/2¼ lbs body weight.

The ingredients in this recipe can be divided into daily portions

Morning: porridge

At noon: part of the rice, supplemented with vegetables and one third of the chicken meat.

Evening: the rest of the chicken with rice and lettuce. The meal supplies all necessary nutrients if you add essential minerals and vitamins.

Chicken can also be prepared with pasta, but the deficiency of fats must be replaced. In this recipe, it was achieved by adding rolled oats. In Recipe No. 6, the fat comes in the form of lard.

RECIPE No. 6

Chicken, Pasta, Vegetables

For a dog weighing 15 kg/33 lbs:
200 g/7 oz cooked chicken, **200 g/7 oz** pasta, **60 g/2¼ oz** cooked vegetables, ½ teaspoon of lard

Cook the chicken as in the preceding recipe. Cook the rice in the normal way. If you decide to use fresh root vegetables instead of frozen ones, the cooking time will be longer. Remember always to cook them in a covered pan and not to boil them any longer than necessary for the vegetables to soften.

Mix the lard into the strained pasta. Add the meat and vegetables and moisten with the chicken stock. Then watch your friend enjoy his meal.

2 kg/4½ lbs:
30 g/1⅛ oz boneless chicken, **30 g/1⅛ oz** pasta, **10 g/¼ oz** vegetables, small piece of fat (¼ teaspoon).
During the day, half a slice of bread (25 g/1 oz) or 3–5 dog biscuits.

5 kg/11 lbs:
80 g/2⅞ oz boneless chicken, **60 g/2¼ oz** pasta, **30 g/1⅛ oz** vegetables, small piece of fat (¼ teaspoon).

🦴 During the day, half a slice of bread (25 g/1 oz) or 3–5 dog biscuits.

10 kg/22 lbs:
150 g/5½ oz chicken meat, **140 g/5 oz** pasta, **50 g/1¾ oz** vegetables small piece of fat (¼ teaspoon).

15 kg/33 lbs:
200 g/7 oz chicken meat, **200 g/7 oz** pasta, **60 g/2¼ oz** vegetables, 2.5 g fat (about half a teaspoon).

20 kg/44 lbs:
250 g/9 oz chicken meat, **270 g/9¼ oz** pasta, **80 g/2⅞ oz** vegetables, **3 g** lard (just over half a teaspoon).

20–22 kg/44–50 lbs:
10 g/¼ oz chicken meat, **5 g/⅛ oz** pasta, **10 g/¼ oz** vegetables, ¼ teaspoon fat per **1 kg/ 2¼ lbs** of body weight.

Each helping contains the necessary nutritional requirements of proteins, fats and carbohydrates. The calorific value is a little higher in this recipe.

We have already suggested two highly nutritious meals made from chicken. Recipe No. 7 is a third possibility, using chicken in a meal containing less fats, proteins and thus less calories.

RECIPE No. 7

Chicken, Rice, Vegetables

Simply cook the ingredients as per the instructions in the preceeding recipes.

2 kg/4½ lbs:
30 g/1⅛ oz chicken meat, **30 g/1⅛ oz** oz rice, **10 g/¼ oz** vegetables.

5 kg/11 lbs:
70 g/2½ oz chicken meat, **60 g/2¼ oz** rice, **25 g/1 oz** vegetables.

10 kg/22 lbs:
140 g/5 oz chicken meat, **120 g/4¼ oz** rice, **40 g/1½ oz** vegetables.

15 kg/33 lbs:
200 g/7 oz chicken meat, **180 g/6½ oz** rice, **70 g/2½ oz** vegetables.

20 kg/44 lbs:
250 g/9 oz chicken meat, **240 g/8½ oz** rice, **100 g/3½ oz** vegetables.

NOTE If cottage cheese is added to the daily diet according to each weight category (10 g/¼ oz, 20 g /¾ oz, 30 g/1⅛ oz, 45 g/1⅔ oz, 60 g/2¼ oz) the nutritional value of the meal will be enhanced. Cottage cheese is a valuable addition to food as it is rich in proteins and fats.

RECIPE No. 8

Pig's or Ox Heart, Pasta, Dry Dog Food

For a dog weighing 15 kg/33 lbs:
220 g/7½ oz cooked pig's (or ox) heart, **200 g/7 oz** cooked pasta, 1 tablespoon dry dog food.

Cut the heart into quarters, wash it and soak in cold water with a little salt. Heart is a muscle and it needs a longer cooking time. It should be cooked until soft. Mince or chop the cooked heart. Put the dry dog food into the dog's bowl and add a little of the stock. Mix in the chopped heart and the pasta. A mixture of heart and beef or chicken is also suitable (half and half).

Your dog may find this mixture strange at first, but he will get accustomed to these new flavours. After

My goodness — he is eating chicken droppings, dog excreta, rubbish, and he is sick! This demonstrates a lack of proper nutrients, vegetable and mineral substances and vitamins. We had better provide a well-balanced meal quickly!

the changeover to dry dog food, remember your dog will be thirsty and you should keep his water bowl filled to prevent dehydration.

2 kg/4½ lbs:
30 g/1⅛ oz heart, **30 g/1⅛ oz** pasta, 1 tablespoon dry dog food.

5 kg/11 lbs:
75 g/2¾ oz heart, **60 g/2¼ oz** pasta, 1 tablespoon dry dog food.

10 kg/22 lbs:
150 g/5½ oz heart, **140 g/5 oz** pasta, 1 tablespoon dry dog food.

15 kg/33 lbs:
230 g/8¼ oz heart, **200 g/7 oz** pasta, 1 tablespoon dry dog food.

20 kg/44 lbs:
300 g/10½ oz heart, **270 g/9¼ oz** pasta, 1 tablespoon dry dog food.

20–22 kg/44–50 lbs:
10 g/¼ oz of cooked heart, **10 g/¼ oz** pasta, and a little dry dog food per 1 kg/2¼ lbs of body weight.

Ox heart has a lower calorific value than pig's heart, but it has more nutritious fats. We can now prepare a good, nutritious meal with rice.

RECIPE No. 9

Ox (or Pig's) Heart, Rice, Vegetables

For a dog weighing 15 kg/33 lbs:
200 g/7 oz cooked heart, **180 g/6½ oz** cooked rice, **80 g/2⅞ oz** cooked vegetables.

All the constituents of the meal are easy to prepare. It should be said that the protein and fat content and the calorific value are well below the standard requirement. This recipe is suitable for older and obese dogs. Portions can be divided or mixed in with beef.

2 kg/4½ lbs:
30 g/1⅛ oz heart, **25 g/1 oz** rice, **15 g/½ oz** vegetables.

5 kg/11 lbs:
75 g/2¾ oz heart, **60 g/2¼ oz** rice, **30 g/1⅛ oz** vegetables.

10 kg/22 lbs:
150 g/5½ oz heart, **120 g/4¼ oz** rice, **50 g/1¾ oz** vegetables.

15 kg/33 lbs:
200 g/7 oz heart, **180 g/6½ oz** rice, **80 g/2⅞ oz** vegetables.

20 kg/44 lbs:
250 g/9 oz heart, **240 g/8½ oz** rice, **100 g/3½ oz** vegetables.

20–22 kg/44–50 lbs:
10 g/¼ oz of heart, **10 g/¼ oz** of rice, **10 g/¼ oz** of vegetables per 1 kg/2¼ lbs of body weight.

Tripe is a popular dog food and can be bought cheaply. You will certainly appreciate the economy after the lavishness of the previous recipes. What is more, tripe contains suitable amounts of proteins. Fat content is rather low, so lard should be added. Tripe requires long, slow cooking. If you are going to spend so much time preparing it, you might as well make some for yourself as well. After all, tripe is one of the national dishes of Northern England. But be careful, tripe loses half its weight in cooking, so make sure you prepare enough. Pork chitterlings can be prepared in a similar manner.

RECIPE No. 10

Tripe with Pasta and Vegetables

For a dog weighing 15 kg/33 lbs:
230 g/8¼ oz boiled tripe, **200 g/7 oz** pasta, **60 g/2¼ oz** boiled vegetables, 10 g/¼ oz lard.

The tripe should be washed in several changes of water and scrubbed if necessary. Then put it into a pan of slightly salted water. Boil first for half an hour. Then drain off the water and put the tripe into a pan of fresh cold water. Cook it until soft. This may take two hours or more. When soft, drain again, saving the stock, and cut into slices. Then boil the vegetables in the tripe stock. Remember to cook enough for yourself as well.

Put the cooked pasta into a bowl, stir in the lard, tripe and vegetables. Pour a little stock over the dish and serve. Your friend will love it.

Now you can finish cooking your own dinner. Serve the rest of the tripe for yourself in a white sauce. Add boiled vegetables to the sauce, together with the tripe and salt, pepper, marjoram to taste. Boil everything for a short time. After boiling, sprinkle with chopped parsley and serve. Instead of pasta, a bread roll would go well with it.

2 kg/4½ lbs:

30 g/1⅛ oz tripe, **30 g/1⅛ oz** pasta, **10 g/¼ oz** vegetables, 2 g/⅛ teaspoon lard.

🦴 During the day, 1 dog biscuit.

5 kg/11 lbs:

80 g/2⅞ oz tripe, **60 g/2¼ oz** pasta, **50 g/1¾ oz** vegetables, 3 g/¼ teaspoon lard.

🦴 During the day, 1½ dog biscuits.

10 kg/22 lbs:

150 g/5½ oz tripe, **140 g/5 oz** pasta, **50 g/1¾ oz** vegetables, 5 g/⅛ oz lard.

🦴 During the day, 2 dog biscuits.

15 kg/33 lbs:

230 g/8¼ oz tripe, **200 g/7 oz** pasta, **60 g/2¼ oz** vegetables, 10 g/¼ oz lard.

20 kg/44 lbs:

300 g/10½ oz tripe, **270 g/9¼ oz** pasta, **70 g/2½ oz** vegetables, 10 g/¼ oz lard.

If your dog lacks exercise, he will digest bones only with difficulty and serious constipation will result. This could lead to a blockage that might require an operation.

20–22 kg/44–50 lbs:
10 g/¼ oz tripe, **10 g/¼ oz** pasta, **5 g/⅛ oz** vegetables per 1 kg/2¼ lbs of body weight, 10g/¼ oz lard.

All these portions are well balanced.

One of the recipes sent to me by Mr. Kolár may be worth your attention. His dachshund Bondy used to love liver but always suffered from diarrhoea after it. That problem led to the following recipe.

RECIPE No. 11

Beef, Pig's Liver, Pasta, Vegetables, Rolled Oats

For a dog weighing 15 kg/33 lbs:

110 g/3¾ oz boiled beef (forequarter), **110 g/3¾ oz** boiled pig's liver, **200 g/7 oz** boiled pasta, **60 g/2¼ oz** boiled root vegetables, ½ level teaspoon of lard, 2 heaped tablespoons of rolled oats.

While the beef is boiling, prepare the rest of the ingredients. Wash the liver and add it to the boiled meat 10–15 minutes before the end of cooking time. If you prefer, cook the liver separately.

When this is ready, sprinkle with 2 tablespoons of dry wheat flakes or rolled oats. Moisten with a ladle of the hot stock. Mix ½ level teaspoon of fat into the cooked pasta, stir in the vegetables and meat mixture. Bondy loves it.

2 kg/4½ lbs:

15 g/½ oz meat, **15 g/½ oz** liver, **30 g/1⅛ oz** pasta, **10 g/¼ oz** vegetables, 1 rounded teaspoon rolled oats, ¼ teaspoon lard.

5 kg/11 lbs:

40 g/1½ oz meat, **40 g/1½ oz** liver, **60 g/2¼ oz** pasta, **25 g/1 oz** vegetables, 1 rounded tablespoon rolled oats, ¼ teaspoon lard.

10 kg/22 lbs:
75 g/2¾ oz meat, 75 g/2¾ oz liver, 135 g/4¾ oz pasta, 50 g/1¾ oz vegetables, 1½ tablespoons rolled oats, ¼ teaspoon lard.

15 kg/33 lbs:
110 g/3¾ oz meat, 110 g/3¾ oz liver, 195 g/6¾ oz pasta, 60 g/2¼ oz vegetables, 2 tablespoons rolled oats, ½ level teaspoon lard.

20 kg/44 lbs:
145 g/5¼ oz meat, 145 g/5¼ oz liver, 270 g/9¼ oz pasta, 70 g/2½ oz vegetables, 2½ tablespoons rolled oats, ½ level teaspoon lard.

20–22 kg/44–50 lbs:
5 g/⅛ oz meat, 5 g/⅛ oz liver, 10 g/¼ oz pasta, 10 g/¼ oz vegetables, 1 teaspoon rolled oats and ¼ teaspoon lard per 1 kg/2¼ lbs of body weight.

Do not use rice instead of pasta as rice is too low in fats. We compensated for this in our recipes by adding lard. If you prefer to use rice, then mix it with porridge. The food ration for dogs weighing over 10 kg/22 lbs loses some of the necessary proteins. This problem can be solved by adding cheese and by reducing the proportion of liver. Try it.

RECIPE No. 12

Beef, Pig's Liver, Porridge, Rice, Processed Cheese

For a dog weighing 15 kg/33 lbs:

140 g/5 oz boiled beef (forequarter), **70 g/2½ oz** boiled pig's liver, **120 g/4¼ oz** rolled oats, **80 g/2⅞ oz** boiled rice, 40 g/1½ oz processed cheese.

Prepare the beef and liver in the same way as for Recipe No. 11. Cook the rice and oats in the method described in Recipe No. 5.

Stir the processed cheese into the mixture just before the oats are cooked. The low protein problem has been solved by adding cheese. The mixture can be improved by the addition of parsley or lettuce. And again remember to add mineral and vitamin supplements.

2 kg/4½ lbs:

20 g/¾ oz meat, **10 g/¼ oz** liver, **25 g/1 oz** porridge, **10 g/¼ oz** rice, 5 g/⅛ oz cheese.

5 kg/11 lbs:

50 g/1¾ oz meat, **30 g/1⅛ oz** liver, **50 g/1¾ oz** porridge, **30 g/1⅛ oz** rice, 10 g/¼ oz cheese.

10 kg/22 lbs:
100 g/3½ oz meat, 50 g/1¾ oz liver, 75 g/2¾ oz porridge, **60 g/2¼ oz** rice, 20 g/¾ oz cheese.

15 kg/33 lbs:
140 g/5 oz meat, **70 g/2½ oz** liver, **120 g/4¼ oz** porridge, **80 g/2⅞ oz** rice, 40 g/1½ oz cheese.

20 kg/44 lbs:
180 g/6½ oz meat, **100 g/3½ oz** liver, **150 g/5½ oz** porridge, **90 g /3¼ oz** rice, 60 g/2¼ oz cheese.

20–22 kg/44–50 lbs:
10 g/¼ oz meat, **5 g/⅛ oz** liver, **5 g/⅛ oz** porridge, **5 g/⅛ oz** rice for every 1 kg/2¼ lbs of body weight. Plus 80 g/2⅞ oz cottage cheese.

Fish fillet or other types of fish should be a frequent item in a dog's menu.

RECIPE No. 13

Fish Fillet, Rice, Carrots, Cottage Cheese

For a dog weighing 15 kg/33 lbs:
230 g/8¼ oz boiled fish fillet, **180 g/6½ oz** boiled rice, 50 g/1¾ oz grated raw carrot, 120 g/4¼ oz soft cottage cheese.

Wash the fish fillet, then put it into cold water with several drops of vinegar. Simmer for 5–8 minutes. Drain the fillet and carefully search for and remove the bigger bones. Add the boiled rice and pour the fish stock over it.

This dish is not well-balanced for the average dog's needs, especially as regards fat content. However with the addition of boiled carrot it is suitable as a diet for sick, old or obese dogs. In order to make up this deficiency, I

> NOTE The fish can also be steamed. Place it in a little butter and water, and cook on both sides for 4–5 minutes. In this way it will retain more of its nutritional value. To moisten it, use stock made from the carrot or rice water. If you prefer to use pasta as a supplement, by all means do so but reduce the portion of cottage cheese by one half.

recommend adding grated raw carrot to cottage cheese and giving it to the dog soon after his fish meal or even during the day (the weight of the food will be greater).

2 kg/4½ lbs:
40 g/1½ oz boiled fish fillet, **25 g/1 oz** rice, 10 g/¼ oz carrot.
🦴 during the day, 20 g/¾ oz cottage cheese.

5 kg/11 lbs:
80 g/2⅞ oz fish fillet, **60 g/2¼ oz** rice, 25 g/1 oz carrot.
🦴 during the day, 20 g/¾ oz soft cottage cheese.

10 kg/22 lbs:
150 g/5½ oz fish fillet, **120 g/4¼ oz** rice, 40 g/1½ oz carrot.
🦴 during the day, 80 g/2⅞ oz soft cottage cheese.

15 kg/33 lbs:
230 g/8¼ oz fish fillet, **180 g/6½ oz** rice, 50 g/1¾ oz carrot.
🦴 during the day, 120 g/4¼ oz soft cottage cheese.

20 kg/44 lbs:
300 g/10½ oz fish fillet, **240 g/8½ oz** rice, 50 g/1¾ oz carrot.
🦴 during the day, 160 g/5¾ oz soft cottage cheese.

20–22 kg/44–50 lbs:
15 g/½ oz fish fillet, **10 g/¼ oz** rice, 5 g/⅛ oz carrot, 10 g/¼ oz cottage cheese for each additional kg/2¼ lbs of body weight.

A favourite alternative to white fish fillet is boiled mackerel. It is richer in fats, especially when steamed. The protein content is also slightly higher. In this recipe you can add pasta.

RECIPE No. 14

Steamed Mackerel, Pasta, Root Vegetables

For a dog weighing 15kg/33 lbs:
230 g/8½ oz steamed mackerel, **200 g/7 oz** boiled pasta, **50 g/1¾ oz** boiled root vegetables.

Clean the mackerel and cut it into small pieces. Poach in butter and a little water, keeping the pan tightly covered. After 4 minutes, turn over and poach for another four minutes. Pasta and frozen vegetables can be boiled at the same time. Remove as many bones as possible from the mackerel and mix with the boiled pasta and vegetables. Pour a little vegetable stock over the dish.

Don't deprive yourself of tasty mackerel (or fish fillet) either. So cook some extra for yourself. Your own

Do not forget that dogs over the age of ten have a slower digestion. They should therefore be given food that is less rich and in smaller quantities. Divide the meal into several portions to be given throughout the day.

portion of mackerel would be improved by the addition of Hollandaise sauce. Separate 4 eggs, put the yolks into a small bowl and add 200 ml/7 fl oz vegetable stock (if not enough add water). Add 15 g /½ oz butter and a little salt and whisk over a saucepan of hot water. When thick, add a few drops of lemon juice. Pour this sauce over the mackerel and serve warm with bread. White wine can be substituted for lemon juice. Sprinkle with chopped parsley before serving.

2 kg/4½ lbs:
30 g/1⅛ oz mackerel, **30 g/1⅛ oz** pasta, **10 g/¼ oz** vegetables.

5 kg/11 lbs:
80 g/2⅞ oz mackerel, **60 g/2¼ oz** pasta, **30 g/1⅛ oz** vegetables.

Pay attention to your dog's stools. If they are soft but hold a shape and brown or light brown – everything is OK. But if they are hard and crumbly, this means that you have been giving him too many bones. Also, black stools mean too much meat, dry stools mean too little liquid (water), and if he has pulpy stools reduce the supplementary food.

10 kg/22 lbs:
150 g/5½ oz mackerel, **140 g/5 oz** pasta, **40 g/1½ oz** vegetables.

15 kg/33 lbs:
230 g/8¼ oz mackerel, **200 g/7 oz** pasta, **50 g/1¾ oz** vegetables.

20 kg/44 lbs:
290 g/10 oz mackerel, **270 g/9¼ oz** pasta, **60 g/2¼ oz** vegetables.

20–22 kg/44–50 lbs:
10 g/¼ oz mackerel, **10 g/¼ oz** pasta, **10 g/¼ oz** vegetables for each
1 kg/2¼ lbs body weight.

This meal contains all the necessary food values.
However, for dogs weighing under 10 kg/22 lbs, it is
not quite so nutritious and can be supplemented with a
piece of stale bread roll or a few dog biscuits. The ration
for the higher weight categories (from 15 kg/33 lbs) is
richer in calories (500–800 kJ/2100–3360 kCal or
more). Those calories will come in useful after exercise.
Mackerel can also be minced with its bones in a food
processor.

Kidneys are a popular ingredient for dogs. The following
two recipes are from Mrs. Stêdrá.

RECIPE No. 15

Pig's Kidneys, Pasta, Vegetables

For a dog weighing 15 kg/33 lbs:

250 g/9 oz fried pig's kidney, **200 g/7 oz** cooked pasta, **40 g/1½ oz** boiled root vegetables, fat for frying, ½ small chopped onion, ¼ teaspoon lard. For yourself you will need an extra portion of kidney and more onion.

As you will be preparing this food both for yourself and your dog, you should be very careful to clean the meat thoroughly. Cut the kidney lengthways, remove the fat and gristle and wash the kidney well. Dry on a kitchen towel and cut into 2 mm/⅛ inch thick slices. Put the fat in a frying pan, add the chopped onion and meat and cook for about two minutes until pale in colour. Separate a portion for your dog.

At this stage the dog's meat is ready and it can be served with boiled pasta and vegetables. Do not forget to pour some vegetable stock over it, but ensure the mixture is not too wet or soupy. Now you can complete your own dinner. Return the remaining kidneys to the frying-pan, sprinkle with flour then add a little vegetable stock. Season with pepper, adding salt to taste just before serving. Serve with bread rolls, rice or pasta.

2 kg/4½ lbs:
30 g/1⅛ oz kidneys, **30 g/1⅛ oz** pasta, **10 g/¼ oz** root vegetables, ¼ small chopped onion, fat for frying, ⅛ teaspoon fat for the pasta.

5 kg/11 lbs:
90 g/3¼ oz kidneys, **80 g/2⅞ oz** pasta, **20 g/¾ oz** root vegetables ¼ small chopped onion, fat for frying, ¼ teaspoon fat for the pasta.

10 kg/22 lbs:
170 g/6 oz kidneys, **140 g/5 oz** pasta, **30 g/1⅛ oz** root vegetables, ¼ small chopped onion, fat for frying, ¼ teaspoon fat for the pasta.

15 kg/33 lbs:
250 g/9 oz kidneys, **200 g/7 oz** pasta, **40 g/1½ oz** root vegetables, ¼ small chopped onion, fat for frying, ¼ teaspoon fat for the pasta.

20 kg/44 lbs:
320 g/11 oz kidneys, **270 g/9¼ oz** pasta, **50 g/1¾ oz** root vegetables, ¼ small chopped onion, fat for frying, ½ teaspoon fat for the pasta.

20–22 kg/44–50 lbs:
10 g/¼ oz kidneys, **5 g/⅛ oz** pasta, **10 g/¼ oz** root vegetables for each 1 kg/2¼ lbs body weight. Plus ½ teaspoon fat for the pasta and fat for the frying.

There is a higher calorific value in the meals for the higher weight categories (over 15 kg/33 lbs). This will not harm an active dog. A less active dog should not have fat added to his food. For weights up to 15 kg/33 lbs, this recipe is a little low in calories. Add a piece of bread roll or wholemeal bread to provide additional calories.

While on the subject of kidneys, ox kidneys contain less protein than pig's kidneys but have more fat and calories. Once again the following recipe can be used for yourself as well.

RECIPE No. 16

Ox Kidneys, Rice, Hard Cheese (for grating), Fat

For a dog weighing 15 kg/33 lbs:
250 g/9 oz fried kidneys, **180 g/6½ oz** boiled rice, 45 g/1⅔ oz yellow cheese, fat for frying, ½ small coarsely chopped onion.

The Ox kidneys (or pig's kidneys) are prepared in the same way as in the previous recipe.

Grate the cheese and add it to the boiled rice. Add the chopped, cooked meat and stir the mixture well. It is a good idea to add a little chopped lettuce or chives. Pour beef stock, if any, or rice water containing part of a beef stock cube over the food.

Remember the rule from the chapter about serving food. Your dog should be fed before you eat. So, now he is eating, there is time to finish preparing your dinner. Proceed according to Recipe No. 15.

2 kg/4½ lbs:
30 g/1⅛ oz kidneys, **30 g/1⅛ oz** rice, 10 g/¼ oz cheese, ¼ small onion, fat for frying the onion.

🦴 during the day, 2–3 dog biscuits.

5 kg/11 lbs:
90 g/3¼ oz kidneys, **60 g/2¼ oz** rice, 15 g/½ oz cheese, ¼ small chopped onion and fat for frying the onion.

🦴 during the day, for a slim dog: 4–5 dog biscuits.

10 kg/22 lbs:
170 g/6 oz kidneys, **120 g/4¼ oz** rice, 35 g/1¼ oz cheese, ½ small chopped onion, fat for frying the onion.

15 kg/33 lbs:
250 g/9 oz kidneys, **180 g/6½ oz** rice, 45 g/1⅔ oz cheese, ½ small chopped onion, fat for frying the onion.

20 kg/44 lbs:
320 g/11 oz kidneys, **240 g/8½ oz** rice, 65 g/2⅓ oz cheese, 1 small chopped onion, fat for frying the onion.

20–22 kg/44–50 lbs:
10 g/¼ oz kidneys, **5 g/⅛ oz** rice, 10 g/¼ oz cheese for every 1 kg /2¼ lbs of body weight, plus 1 small chopped onion, fat for frying.

This recipe is rich in calories and fats. It is suitable for dogs who are able to run about in the open air such as hunting dogs, dogs in training etc.

By eliminating the grated cheese and substituting vegetables, the calorific value will be reduced to the normal level but the protein content will be less than normal. The recipe thus becomes suitable for older dogs or for a dog to eat after high-protein foods (such as chicken with pasta, steamed mackerel etc.). Kidneys can be combined with beef (half and half).

Minced beef is a very acceptable and easily digested food for our friend as you will see if you try out the following recipes.

RECIPE No. 17

Minced Beef (forequarter), Pasta, Vegetables

For a dog weighing 15 kg/33 lbs:
230 g/8¼ oz boiled minced beef, **200 g/7 oz** boiled pasta, **50 g/1¾ oz** boiled root vegetables.

You may be surprised at the unusual preparation method but it is easy and quick.

Pour cold, slightly salted water over the minced beef and bring it to the boil. The foam which appears on the surface should be mixed in. After boiling point has been reached, cook the meat for 2–3 minutes. Pour off some of the stock. Then add the cooked pasta and the cooked vegetables. Put the mixture into your friend's bowl and wait for his approval.

This food is easily digested and therefore may be served to an older dog. It can be easily divided into portions. Do not forget the mineral and vitamin supplements.

2 kg/4½ lbs:
40 g/1½ oz mince, **30 g/1⅛ oz** pasta, **10 g/¼ oz** root vegetables.

5 kg/11 lbs:
100 g/3½ oz mince, **60 g/2¼ oz** pasta, **20 g/¾ oz** root vegetables.
🦴 During the day, hard cheese (15 g/½ oz).

10 kg/22 lbs:
170 g/6 oz mince, **140 g/5 oz** pasta, **30 g/1⅛ oz** root vegetables.
🦴 During the day, hard cheese (20 g/¾ oz).

15 kg/33 lbs:
230 g/8¼ oz mince, **200 g/7 oz** pasta, **50 g/1¾ oz** vegetables.
🦴 During the day, hard cheese (25 g/1 oz).

20 kg/44 lbs:
300 g/10½ oz mince, **250 g/9 oz** pasta, **60 g/2¼ oz** vegetables.
🦴 During the day, hard cheese (25 g/1 oz).

20–22 kg/44–50 lbs:
10 g/¼ oz mince, **5 g/⅛ oz** pasta, **10 g/¼ oz** vegetables for every 1 kg/2¼ lbs of body weight and a little hard cheese during the day.

RECIPE No 18

Minced Beef (forequarter), Rice, Vegetables

For a dog weighing 15 kg/33lbs:
220 g/7½ oz boiled minced beef, **180 g/6½ oz** rice, **60 g/2¼ oz** root vegetables.

The boiled rice should be added to the boiled minced beef followed by mashed boiled vegetables. Pour over a little vegetable stock, mix well and serve to your impatient little friend.

2 kg/4½ lbs:
30 g/1⅛ oz minced beef, **30 g/1⅛ oz** rice, **10 g/¼ oz** vegetables.

5 kg/11 lbs:
75 g/2¾ oz minced beef, **60 g/2¼ oz** rice, **20 g/¾ oz** vegetables.

> NOTE This recipe appeared frequently in response to our questionnaire, but because it contains less protein, fats and calories it is insufficient for the main, daily meal. In our kitchen, too, it is definitely a favourite, but we enrich it with egg and hard cheese and thus it becomes a balanced and nutritious meal.

10 kg/22 lbs:
150 g/5½ oz minced beef, **120 g/4¼ oz** rice, **40 g/1½ oz** vegetables.

15 kg/33 lbs:
220 g/7½ oz minced beef, **180 g/6½ oz** rice, **60 g/2¼ oz** vegetables.

20 kg/44 lbs:
290 g/10 oz minced beef, **240 g/8½ oz** rice, **80 g/2⅞ oz** vegetables.

20–22 kg/44–50 lbs:
10 g/¼ oz minced beef, **10 g/¼ oz** rice, **10 g/¼ oz** vegetables for every 1 kg/2¼ lbs of body weight.

You should cut down occasionally on high-protein ingredients. Food for older dogs can be divided into several portions. It can be wrapped in foil and re-heated in the oven or wrapped in clingfilm and reheated in the microwave oven. After heating, add some vegetable stock.

To retain both the original weight of raw minced meat and thus most of the important nutrients, try the following recipe.

RECIPE No. 19

Baked Minced Beef (forequarter), Pasta, Cheese, Egg, Raw Carrot

For a dog weighing 15 kg/33 lbs:
170 g/6 oz baked minced beef, **180 g/6½ oz** pasta (spaghetti), one egg, 30 g/1⅛ oz grated cheese, 50 g/1¾ oz cooked or raw grated carrot.

Minced meat can also be prepared in this way*: put a little oil or stock into a pan and add the minced meat. During cooking, use a wooden spoon to break up large lumps into little pieces which are then mixed into the cooked spaghetti. (Do not forget to chop the spaghetti). There are two ways in which to continue. You can either add cheese cut into cubes together with boiled grated carrot or add an egg beaten in hot vegetable stock. You may require extra stock.

The second way gives more work but eliminates having to use a raw egg. Grease an ovenproof glass dish or saucepan with margarine or lard and sprinkle with breadcrumbs. Fill with a mixture of minced meat and

---

* This method of cooking reduces the weight of the meat very little. It could also be used in Recipe Nos. 17 or 18 without increasing the amounts by one third.

chopped cooked spaghetti. Sprinkle with grated cheese and pour the beaten egg over it. Bake in a hot oven. If you add minced meat, spaghetti, cheese and two eggs, you will have your own dinner too.

Serve a portion to your dog. Add a little raw carrot and break up the meal in his bowl.

Your own dinner will need salt and can be served with ketchup.

2 kg/4½ lbs:
20 g/¾ oz minced meat, **30 g/1⅛ oz** pasta, half egg, 5 g/⅛ oz cheese, **10 g/¼ oz** carrot.

5 kg/11 lbs:
60 g/2¼ oz minced beef, **60 g/2¼ oz** pasta, one egg, 10 g/¼ oz cheese, **30 g/1⅛ oz** carrot.

We do our friend no favours by giving him more nutrients in his food than he really needs. It upsets his digestion, he will pass some of the nutrients in his stools and he will weigh more than he should.

Moreover dog biscuits should not be served as a daily routine, but only as a special treat.

10 kg/22 lbs:
120 g/4¼ oz minced beef, **140 g/5 oz** pasta, one egg, 10 g/¼ oz cheese, **40 g/1½ oz** carrot.

15 kg/33 lbs:
170 g/6 oz minced beef, **180 g/6½ oz** pasta, one egg, 30 g/1⅛ oz cheese, **50 g/1¾ oz** carrot.

20 kg/44 lbs:
180 g/6½ oz minced beef, **225 g/8 oz** pasta, two eggs, 40 g/1½ oz cheese, **60 g/2½ oz** carrot.

20–22 kg/44–50 lbs:
10 g/¼ oz mince, **10 g/¼ oz** pasta, **2 g/¹⁄₁₆ oz** cheese, **10 g/¼ oz** carrot, for each kg/2¼ lbs of body weight. Two eggs, not more.

This food is richer in proteins and fat. It is suitable for more active dogs.

A dog shall not live by meat alone. Dairy products are also a very important part of his nutrition. Cheese and cottage cheese are especially good sources of proteins and fats.

Do not forget to take them out of the refrigerator in good time. Cold food has no place in a dog's bowl.

RECIPE No.20

Cottage Cheese, Wholemeal Bread, Hard Cheese

For a dog weighing 15 kg/33 lbs:

200 g/7 oz cottage cheese, 100 g/3½ oz wholemeal bread, 100 g/3½ oz hard cheese, 2–3 dog biscuits.

Pour a little milk over the cottage cheese to thin it down. Two slices of bread (stale is preferable) should be grated or crumbled in a food processor. Use a cheese that is not too salty and cut it into cubes. Add crushed dog biscuits. Do not leave these out because they replace the slight loss of proteins and calories. Mix thoroughly. Our friend can now eat his dinner and we can take a rest.

2 kg/4½ lbs:

30 g/1⅛ oz cottage cheese, 20 g/¾ oz wholemeal bread, 10 g/¼ oz hard cheese, 4 dog biscuits.

5 kg/11 lbs:

80 g/2⅞ oz cottage cheese, 50 g/1¾ oz wholemeal bread, 30 g/1⅛ oz hard cheese, 7 dog biscuits.

10 kg/22 lbs:

130 g/4½ oz cottage cheese, 75 g/2¾ oz wholemeal bread, 60 g/2¼ oz hard cheese, 8 dog biscuits.

15 kg/33 lbs:

200 g/7 oz cottage cheese, 100 g/3½ oz wholemeal bread, 100 g/3½ oz hard cheese, 8 dog biscuits.

20 kg/44 lbs:

250 g/9 oz cottage cheese, 125 g/4⅓ oz wholemeal bread, 140 g/ 5 oz hard cheese, 7 dog biscuits.

20–22 kg/44lbs–50 lbs:

10 g/¼ oz cottage cheese, 10 g/¼ oz wholemeal bread, 10 g/¼ oz hard cheese for each kg/2¼ lbs of body weight. No dog biscuits.

The recipe, though balanced, has a high content of fat in all weight categories although the level will depend on the quality of the cheese.

The better I know people,
the more I love dogs

No dog gets fat just by licking

RECIPE No. 21

Fruit Yoghurt, Wholemeal Bread, Hard Cheese

For a dog weighing 15 kg/33 lbs:

160 g/5¾ oz fruit yoghurt, 100 g/3½ oz wholemeal bread, 40 g/1½ oz hard cheese.

The method is the same as in Recipe No. 20.

2 kg/4½ lbs:

1½ tablespoons fruit yoghurt, 20 g/¾ oz wholemeal bread, 10 g/¼ oz hard cheese

5 kg/11 lbs:

60 g/2¼ oz yoghurt, 50 g/1¾ oz wholemeal bread, 20 g/¾ oz hard cheese.

10 kg/22 lbs:

120 g/4¼ oz fruit yoghurt, 75 g/2¾ oz wholemeal bread, 30 g/1⅛ oz cheddar cheese.

Your dog is eating grass! This is not a forecast of rainy weather, as some would have it, but indicates that the dog is suffering from a lack of vegetables and fibre.

---

15 kg/33 lbs:

160 g/5¾ oz fruit yoghurt, 100 g/3½ oz wholemeal bread, 40 g/1½ oz hard cheese

20 kg/44 lbs:

200 g/7 oz fruit yoghurt, 125 g/4⅓ oz wholemeal bread, 50 g/1¾ oz hard cheese

20–22 kg/44–50 lbs:

A little yoghurt, bread and cheese for every kg/2¼ lbs of body weight.

All the ingredients in the recipe have lower nutritional values, especially of proteins and carbohydrates. It also contains one third less calories. Fats are equally reduced. Use this meal during one-day fasts when you feel very sorry for your dog and can't bear his whining.

You can also use the following recipe as a pacifier.

NOTE Instead of wholemeal bread you may use rye bread or a wholemeal bread roll.

RECIPE No. 22

Wholemeal Bread, Processed Cheese, Buttermilk or Yoghurt

For a dog weighing 15 kg/33 lbs

100 g/3½ oz wholemeal bread, 80 g/2⅞ oz processed cheese, 200 ml/ 7 fl oz buttermilk or natural yoghurt.

Spread two slices of bread with cheese. The thickness depends on you. Cut into squares. Pour the sour milk over them and mix well. Hairy dogs should have the remains of the milk wiped off their beards.

2 kg/4½ lbs:

20 g/¾ oz wholemeal bread, 15 g/½ oz processed cheese, 50 ml/2 fl oz buttermilk or yoghurt.

Never give your friend cakes, chocolate or sweets. They are a very harmful habit. As a reward (mainly as praise) use a dog biscuit. This is quite sufficient.

After dinner, I recommend giving your friend a dog biscuit, a slice of bread or a piece of apple or carrot to clean his teeth, just as we do with children.

---

5 kg/11 lbs:

50 g/1¾ oz wholemeal bread, 30 g/1⅛ oz processed cheese, 50 ml/ 2 fl oz buttermilk or yoghurt

10 kg/22 lbs:

75 g/2¾ oz wholemeal bread, 60 g/2¼ oz processed cheese, 150 ml/ 5 fl oz (G pint) buttermilk or yoghurt.

15 kg/33 lbs:

100 g/3½ oz wholemeal bread, 80 g/2⅞ oz processed cheese, 200 ml/ 7 fl oz buttermilk or yoghurt.

20 kg/44 lbs:

125 g/4⅓ oz wholemeal bread, 100 g/3½ oz processed cheese, 250 ml/9 fl oz buttermilk or yoghurt.

20–22 kg/44–50 lbs:

10 g/¼ oz wholemeal bread, 2 g/¹⁄₁₆th oz processed cheese, buttermilk or yoghurt according to need for every 1 kg/2¼ lbs of body weight.

This meal is lower in calories especially for the 10 kg/22 lbs and upwards category of dog.

We have used rolled oats in previous recipes as a supplement. Slightly enriched, they can be used as the daily meal.

RECIPE No.23

Porridge, Apple, Hard Cheese

For a dog weighing 15 kg/33 lbs:
220 g/7½ oz porridge, **100 g/3½ oz** grated apple, 120 g/4¼ oz hard cheese.

Make the porridge and mix it with the grated apple. Cut the cheese into cubes and add it. Mix everything thoroughly and then serve.

2 kg/4½ lbs:
30 g/1⅛ oz porridge, 25 g/1 oz apple, 15 g/½ oz hard cheese.
during the day, 3–4 dog biscuits.

5 kg/11 lbs:
90 g/3¼ oz porridge, 50 g/1¾ oz apple, 40 g/1½ oz hard cheese
during the day, 3–4 dog biscuits.

Never put meat that has gone off, or mouldy or fermenting food into your dog's bowl...
    Kitchen waste is not suitable for dog food!

10 kg/22 lbs:
170 g/6 oz porridge, 70 g/2½ oz apple, 70 g/2½ oz hard cheese
🦴 during the day, 5–6 dog biscuits.

15 kg/33 lbs:
220 g/7½ oz porridge, 100 g/3½ oz apple, 120 g/4¼ oz hard cheese
🦴 during the day, 7–8 dog biscuits.

20 kg/44 lbs:
270 g/9¼ oz porridge, 150 g/5½ oz apple, 160 g/5¾ oz hard cheese
🦴 during the day, 8–10 dog biscuits.

20–22 kg/44–50 lbs:
10 g/¼ oz porridge, 10 g/¼ oz hard cheese, 10 g/¼ oz grated apple for each 1 kg/2¼ lbs of body weight.

This meal is rich in fats (cheese), sometimes almost double the norm. The apple slightly raises the carbohydrate level and the porridge makes the food high in calories. It is good for dogs during cold weather or on days of high activity in autumn or spring.

Soya flakes may also be given to your dog as in the following recipes. They are rich in proteins and fats, but their calorific value is quite low. It is a good idea to mix them with porridge which are richer in proteins.

RECIPE No. 24

Soya and Porridge with Added Vegetables

For a dog weighing 15 kg/33 lbs:
120 g/4¼ oz raw soya flakes, **150 g/5½ oz** porridge with the addition of 80 g/2⅞ oz grated or boiled carrot, boiled root vegetables, raspberries, strawberries, tomatoes.

Mix the raw soya flakes* into the cooked oats. Add chosen vegetables or fruit.

2 kg/4½ lbs:
15 g/½ oz soya flakes **20 g/¾ oz** porridge, 20 g/¾ oz fruit or vegetables.

5 kg/11 lbs:
40 g/1½ oz soya flakes, **50 g/1¾ oz** porridge, 40 g/1½ oz fruit or vegetables.

10 kg/22 lbs:
80 g/2⅞ oz soya flakes, **100 g/3½ oz** porridge, 60 g/2¼ oz fruit or vegetables

* Raw soya flakes should be served only occasionally and in small amounts. They take longer to digest.

15 kg/33 lbs:

120 g/4¼ oz soya flakes, **150 g/5½ oz** porridge, 80 g/2⅞ oz fruit or vegetables.

20 kg/44 lbs:

150 g/5½ oz soya flakes, **200 g/7 oz** porridge, 100 g/3½ oz fruit or vegetables.

20–22 kg/44–50 lbs:

10 g/¼ oz soya flakes, **10 g/¼ oz** porridge for each 1 kg/2¼ lbs of body weight. Add vegetables and fruit as you choose.

Your efforts will have resulted in a meal with a slightly higher than normal protein content and a higher carbohydrate content, thanks to the vegetables and fruit. The energy value is 300–600 kJ/1260–2520 kCal below normal.* However, you can serve this meal after high-calorie food or to less active dogs.

We will continue with a recipe containing soya and oats, but the meal will be richer.

* The value can be increased by adding cottage cheese, served during the day.

Recipe No. 25

Porridge and Soya Flakes, Boiled Egg and Cream Cheese with Dog Biscuits

For a dog weighing 15 kg/33 lbs:
150 g/5½ oz rolled oats, 60 g/2¼ oz soya flakes, 2 eggs, ¾ carton cream cheese, 4–5 dog biscuits.

You will see at first glance that the 'balancing' element will be a 'dessert' of cream cheese and dog biscuits.

Mix the porridge and soya flakes. Hard-boil the eggs and chop them into little pieces. Crush the shells in a food processor and add them to the mash together with the eggs. Add a little milk to make a better mash.

After the meal, serve as a dessert: cream cheese and broken dog biscuits with a drop of fruit juice. Give this to less-active dogs during the day.

2 kg/4½ lbs:
25 g/1 oz rolled oats, 5 g/⅛ oz soya flakes, ½ boiled egg, ⅓ carton cream cheese, 2–3 dog biscuits.

5 kg/11 lbs:
50 g/1¾ oz rolled oats, 20 g/¾ oz soya flakes, 1 boiled egg, ½ carton cream cheese, 4–5 dog biscuits.

10 kg/22 lbs:
100 g/3½ oz rolled oats, 40 g/1½ oz soya flakes, 1 boiled egg, ¾ carton cream cheese, 4–5 dog biscuits.

15 kg/33 lbs:
150 g/5½ oz rolled oats, 60 g/2¼ oz soya flakes, 2 boiled eggs, ¾ carton cream cheese, 4–5 dog biscuits.

20 kg/44 lbs:
200 g/7 oz rolled oats, 90 g/3¼ oz soya flakes, 2 boiled eggs, ¾ carton cream cheese, 4–6 dog biscuits.

20–22 kg/44–50 lbs:
The same as above but add a little more cream cheese.

The meal contains essential nutrients and can be divided into different portions, such as mash with eggs or mash with vegetables (carrots should be grated). The cream cheese and dog biscuits can be served at a different time. It is also rich in fats which makes it especially suitable on cold days particularly for dogs who are active outdoors.

Ten Mini-Recipes

These are intended for fast-days, or as an addition to other meals, especially those lower in calories. The amounts are not specified for each weight category. It is up to you to decide how much to give your dog, and when.

1) Cottage Cheese and Tomato

Combine 100 g/3½ oz cottage cheese and 50 g/1¾ oz tomato purée. Approximate nutritional content*: protein 15 g, fats 15 g, carbohydrates 6.2 g, energy 967 kJ/230 kCal.

* Depending on the quality of the ingredients.

2) Fruit Yoghurt and Muesli

Combine 100 g/3½ oz yoghurt and 4 rounded tablespoons of muesli. Approximate nutritional content: protein 8.6 g, fats 7.4 g, carbohydrates 37.2 g, energy 1024 kJ/244 kCal.

3) Yoghurt and Cornflakes

100 g/3½ oz natural yoghurt, 30 g/1⅛ oz cornflakes. Mix together and add 1 teaspoon of fruit juice. Approximate nutritional content: protein 6.3 g, fats 4.5 g, carbohydrates 17.9 g, energy 761 kJ/181 kCal.

4) Cottage Cheese with Fruit Yoghurt and Grated Carrot

Pour fruit yoghurt over 50 g/1¾ oz cottage cheese and add 50 g

/1¾ oz grated carrot. One tablespoon of rolled oats may be added. Approximate nutritional content: protein 12.8 g, fats 11.4 g, carbohydrates 24.2 g, energy 1050 kJ.

5) Cream Cheese with Strawberries

Cut up 50 g/1¾ oz fresh strawberries and mash with 100–120 g/ 3½–4¼ oz cream cheese.

Approximate nutritional content: proteins 12.4 g, fats 15.5 g, carbohydrates 9.8 g, energy 949 kJ/226 kCal.

6) Yoghurt with Dog Biscuits

Break 10g/¼ oz dog biscuits into small pieces and pour 100 g/3½ oz yoghurt over them.

Approximate nutritional content: proteins 8.7 g, fats 6.5 g, carbohydrates 38.7 g, energy 1052 kJ/250 kCal.

7) Fruit Yoghurt with Cheese

Mix 50 g/1¾ oz hard cheese (or ½ a cheese like Camembert) into some fruit yoghurt.

Approximate nutritional content: proteins 19.3 g, fats 10.1 g, carbohydrates 19.6 g, energy 904 kJ/215 kCal.

8) Yoghurt with Boiled Egg and Lettuce

Chop the boiled egg and shred 2 lettuce leaves (or alternatively use dandelion or nettle leaves). Put into a bowl and mix with yoghurt.

Approximate nutritional content: proteins 12.2 g, fats 10 g, carbohydrates 9.7 g, energy 752 kJ/180 kCal.

9) Rice with Boiled Vegetables and Cheese

Combine **100 g/3½ oz** boiled rice and **50 g/1¾ oz** boiled root vegetables. Add 20 g/¾ oz hard cheese cut into cubes.

Approximate nutritional content: proteins 16.1 g, fats 3.5 g, carbohydrates 86 g, energy 1868 kJ/444 kCal.

10) Pasta with Egg and Hard Cheese

Melt a small piece of fat in a pan and add **150 g/5½ oz** boiled pasta. Whisk an egg in a cup with 20 g/¾ oz grated hard cheese. Then follow the method used for scrambling eggs.

Approximate nutritional content: proteins 31.8 g, fats 12.7 g, carbohydrates 109.3 g, energy 2975 kJ/708 kCal.

A Weekly Menu

Some of you are used to following a regular schedule of meals for your dog, perhaps for a week, with an occasional variation. Here is an example of a weekly menu. Adjust according to your own experience and the ingredients to hand.

Friday – beef, rice and vegetables (Recipe No. 1). Cook a double portion of meat (see Sunday).

Saturday – chicken (Recipes Nos. 5 and 6), minced beef (Recipes Nos. 17 and 18).

Sunday – boiled beef, the second half of Friday's meal (Recipe No. 2). The only thing left to do is to prepare a fresh food supplement, such as pasta.

Monday* – an oat-based meal of your choice.

Tuesday – beef (poorer quality) with supplement (Recipe No. 3).

Wednesday – dairy day (Recipes Nos. 20, 21, 22).
Bitches after being on heat and possibly pregnant should be given fish or minced meat (Recipes Nos. 14 and 17 but without the cheese).

Thursday – offal (Recipes Nos. 8, 9, 10, 11).

Friday – we are back to beef (Recipe No. 1).**

You can give your best friend a piece of hard, stale bread first thing in the morning every day. At lunchtime, you can also treat him to a stale roll or a dog biscuit.

* This can be a day of fasting.

** A teaspoonful of oil added to the food twice a week is recommended for small dogs.

Number-Crunch With Us

All that remains is to make a small excursion into nutritional calculations and learn how to work out the necessary quantities. Then, just for fun, try to work out the amounts needed for your dog in the following recipe:

Minced meat (half beef and half pork), pasta, yellow cheese and vegetables.

Spread out the minced meat in a dry frying pan and cook, stirring quickly to break up any lumps. Remove from the heat and stir in the grated cheese. Add the pasta and boiled, chopped vegetables (50 g/1¾ oz). Finally, pour the vegetable stock over the dish.

Now for the mathematics. As an example, take a dog weighing 15 kg/33 lb. It has been shown that the weight of the meal for this weight of dog should be 450 g/ 1 lb. (As usual, this is calculated on the basis of 30 g /1⅛ oz per 1 kg/2¼ lbs of body weight.) We have established that this food should contain 66 g proteins, 19.2 g fats, 151 g carbohydrates and 4305 kJ/960 kCal energy.

To work out the amount of ingredients needed, use the table 'Nutritional and Energy Content in the Recipe Ingredients' on page 91.

Now for the example :

Food	volume	proteins	fats	carbohydrates	energy
	(g)	(g)	(g)	(g)	(kJ)
Minced meat					
(½+½)	220	36.9	16.5	-	1,199
Pasta, boiled	200	26.0	5.8	146	3,200
Cheese	20	5.8	2.9	0.3	216
Total	440	68.7	25.7	146.3	4615
Norm	450	66.0	19.2	151.0	4305
	-10	+2.7	+6.0	-4.7	+310

Now add boiled and mashed frozen vegetables. The weight of the meal will be 50 g/1¾ oz higher but this does not matter. If your dog is not very hungry, the portion can be divided and stored. During the day, give him some grated cheese with boiled vegetables or raw grated carrot. In the evening, he can have minced meat with pasta. Boiled frozen vegetables will only slightly increase the nutritional content.

Try to work out the ideal meal for your own dog (quantity of ingredients and their nutritional content).

NOTE The recipe is richer in fat because of the pork (but that does not matter). If we were to use only beef, the fat and energy content would drop to the norm.

Food	volume (g)	proteins (g)	fats (g)	carbohydrates (g)	energy (kJ)
Minced meat (½+½)					
Pasta, boiled					
Cheese					
Total					
Norm					

+ boiled frozen vegetables.

If you have managed this, why not try to work out the amounts for one of your own recipes? Or let your imagination run riot and create some new and original recipes not to be found in *The Dog's Dinner*.

A well-fed dog will have a shiny coat and a shapely figure. He will demonstrate your culinary skills to the world.

Nutritional and Energy Content in the Recipe Ingredients
(based on 100 g/3½ oz of food)

Food	proteins (g)	fats (g)	carbohydrates (g)	energy (kJ)
Beef, raw	20.0	18.0	-	1100
Beef, cooked	17.3	5.3	-	506
Pork, cooked	16.5	6.3	0.7	453
Minced meat				
(½ beef, ½ pork)	16.8	7.5	-	545
Beef heart	16.5	6.3	0.7	453
Beef liver	19.8	4.2	3.6	570
Beef kidney	15.0	8.1	1.0	587
Tripe	19.1	2.0	-	415
Pork heart	16.9	4.8	0.4	498
Pork kidney	19.6	4.8	2.0	565
Pork fat	-	100.0	-	3,968
Chicken	21.0	5.6	-	590
Fish fillet (cod)	16.5	0.4	-	309
Mackerel	18.7	12.0	-	787
Egg (1 whole)	6.5	5.5	-	330
Egg white	3.7	-	-	65
Egg yolk	2.8	5.5	-	262
Milk (full fat)	3.3	2.5	4.8	250
Cottage cheese*	15.5	15.0	4.0	922

*This depends on the quality of the product.

Food	proteins	fats	carbohydrates	energy
	(g)	(g)	(g)	(kJ)
Yoghurt*	5.7	4.5	9.7	422
Fruit yoghurt*	4.8	3.8	18.7	514
Cream cheese*	12.4	15.0	1.8	802
Processed cheese				
(30% fat cont.)	19.6	11.4	0.8	781
Hard cheese	29.2	14.6	1.8	1,082
Rolled oats, boiled	13.0	7.2	67.8	1,613
Rice boiled	8.2	0.5	79.3	1,521
Pasta boiled	13.0	2.9	73.0	1,600
Potatoes, boiled	2.0	0.1	18.7	355
Soya flour (half-fat)	42.5	6.5	37.2	1,106
Wholemeal bread	6.4	1.0	51.0	1,000
1 dog biscuit	0.3	0.2	2.9	63
Oil (1 tsp)	-	9.8	-	364
Frozen vegetables				
(parsley, carrot)	2.1	0.1	6.4	131
Vegetables, fresh	1.6	0.2	7.1	143
Carrot	1.1	0.2	7.0	150
Lettuce	1.3	0.2	2.2	62.8
Apples	0.3	0.4	15.0	243
Tomatoes	0.9	0.3	4.2	90
Strawberries	0.8	0.5	8.0	147

Under no circumstances!!!

Food	proteins	fats	carbohydrates	energy
	(g)	(g)	(g)	(kJ)
Liver pâté	14.8	31.2	1.9	1,435
Whipped cream	2.4	33.0	2.7	1,275
Pork scratchings	15.5	75.5	-	2.927
Milk chocolate	7.9	32.1	57.0	2,189
Sponge cake or biscuits	7.2	10.1	60.8	1,488

For your recipe

Food	proteins (g)	fats (g)	carbohydrates (g)	energy (kJ)

Total _____

Norm _____

Index

pig's kidneys with pasta, vegetables 58
beef liver with pasta, vegetables, rolled oats 48
beef liver with porridge, rice, processed cheese 50
tripe with pasta and vegetables 45

pasta: with boiled beef, lettuce, rolled oats 27
with minced beef, vegetables 64
with beef, vegetables 30
with chicken, vegetables 38
with steamed mackerel, root vegetables 58
with pig's or ox heart, dry dog food 41
with beef liver, vegetables, rolled oats 48
with pig's kidneys, vegetables 58
with tripe, vegetables 45

porridge: and soya with added vegetables 79
and soya flakes, boiled egg, cream cheese
and dog biscuits 81
with apple, hard cheese 77
with beef liver, rice, processed cheese 50
with chicken, rice 35

My intention was not only to put together a
number of recipes and calculate the various
nutritional and calorific values of their ingredients.
I am also very keen to advocate variety
in your dog's menu, especially
if your imagination can be set
to work to produce some
appealing recipes of your own.